CONTINENTS

NORTH AMERICA

by Emily Koenig

Content Consultant
Edward E. Chatelain
Associate Professor of Geology
Valdosta State University, Georgia

CORE
LIBRARY

Published by ABDO Publishing Company, PO Box 398166, Minneapolis, MN 55439. Copyright © 2014 by Abdo Consulting Group, Inc. International copyrights reserved in all countries. No part of this book may be reproduced in any form without written permission from the publisher. The Core Library™ is a trademark and logo of ABDO Publishing Company.

Printed in the United States of America,
North Mankato, Minnesota
052013
092013

Editor: Blythe Hurley
Series Designer: Becky Daum

Library of Congress Control Number: 2013931975

Cataloging-in-Publication Data
Koenig, Emily C.
  North America / Emily C. Koenig.
    p. cm. -- (Continents)
ISBN 978-1-61783-933-7 (lib. bdg.)
ISBN 978-1-61783-998-6 (pbk.)
1. North America--Juvenile literature.   I. Title.
917--dc23

                                        2013931975

Photo Credits: Caleb Foster/Shutterstock Images, cover, 1; Red Line Editorial, 4, 19, 23; Tim Mainiero/Shutterstock Images, 6; Shutterstock Images, 9, 14, 16, 22, 25, 30, 42 (top), 43 (top), 45; Steve Bower/Shutterstock Images, 12; Eric Gevaert/Shutterstock Images, 20; Gary Saxe/Shutterstock Images, 27; Sergei Bachlakov/Shutterstock Images, 28, 33; Natalia Pushchina/Shutterstock Images, 36; Kike Calvo/AP Images, 38; Andrei Orlov/Shutterstock Images, 40; Kim Seidl/Shutterstock Images, 42 (middle); Songquan Deng/Shutterstock Images, 42 (bottom); Jim Agronick/Shutterstock Images, 43 (middle); Galyna Andrushko/Shutterstock Images, 43 (bottom)

CONTENTS

GREENLAND

Fairbanks

Anchorage

Juneau

CANADA

Edmonton

Calgary

Regina

Winnipeg

Vancouver

Seattle

Quebec

Ottawa

Montreal

Portland

Minneapolis/Saint Paul

Pacific Ocean

UNITED STATES

Detroit

Toronto

Chicago

Cleveland

New York

Salt Lake City

Denver

St. Louis

Philadelphia

Washington DC

San Francisco

Las Vegas

Memphis

Atlantic Ocean

Los Angeles

Atlanta

Dallas

San Antonio

Houston

Miami

MEXICO

Havana

BAHAMAS

CUBA

Guadalajara

Mexico City

JAMAICA

DOMINICAN REPUBLIC

BELIZE

HAITI

HONDURAS

GUATEMALA

EL SALVADOR

NICARAGUA

COSTA RICA

PANAMA

N

QUICK FACTS ABOUT NORTH AMERICA

- **Highest point:** Mt. McKinley, 20,320 feet (6,194 m)

- **Area:** 9,355,000 square miles (24,230,000 sq km)

- **Distance north to south:** Approximately 8,700 miles (14,001 km)

- **Distance east to west:** Approximately 5,000 miles (8,047 km)

- **Key industries:** petroleum, steel, food processing, mining, motor vehicles, natural gas, tourism, telecommunications, electronics

- **Population:** 547,509,565

- **Five biggest cities:** Mexico City, Mexico; New York City, USA; Los Angeles, USA; Chicago, USA; Toronto, Canada

- **Three most common languages:** English, Spanish, French

- **Number of countries:** 23

CHAPTER ONE

INTRODUCING NORTH AMERICA

North America is home to both large cities and unspoiled wilderness. It is our planet's third-largest continent. North America stretches as far north as the Arctic Circle and as far south as Panama.

Canada, the United States, Mexico, and Central America make up mainland North America. Bermuda,

The Blue Ridge Parkway in North Carolina, United States, runs through the Blue Ridge, a major mountain chain that is part of the Appalachian Mountains.

Greenland, the Caribbean Islands, and many other islands are also part of North America.

A Diverse Continent

The countries and people that make up North America are very diverse. But they all share a history of European exploration and colonization. The name *America* comes from an early European explorer named Amerigo Vespucci. Christopher Columbus and Vespucci were some of the first European explorers to come to the Americas.

Today North America is home to many native people. People descended from European immigrants and African slaves also

The Isthmus of Panama

The Isthmus of Panama connects North and South America. It links Panama to South America's Colombia. Many people have traveled between North and South America using the Isthmus of Panama. During the California gold rush of 1849, ships brought people seeking gold from eastern US ports. These people then crossed the isthmus and boarded boats headed for California.

The city of Havana is on the island of Cuba, one of the first North American locations explored by Christopher Columbus.

call it home. The continent's population is constantly changing. People from around the world still immigrate to North America.

A Place Like No Other

North America has many important natural resources. Many North Americans have access to a wealthy lifestyle not found in most other parts of the world. Many people consider the United States to be a

Erik the Red

Erik Thorvaldson founded the first European settlement in North America. Thorvaldson was more commonly known as Erik the Red. He was also the father of Leif Eriksson, one of the first Europeans to explore North America. Erik the Red started his settlement on Greenland in about the year 986. That was more than 500 years before Columbus reached the Americas. By the year 1000, there were approximately 1,000 Scandinavian settlers in Greenland. Historians believe Leif Eriksson reached Nova Scotia, Labrador, and Newfoundland during the early 1000s. He also introduced Christianity to Greenland. His mother built the first church in the New World.

world leader. This is partly because it has the largest economy in the world.

The land is very different from one end of North America to the other. North America's cultures are always changing. Immigration brings new peoples and traditions together. The many people, languages, and landscapes found here make North America different from any other continent on Earth.

Daniel Boone was a hero among settlers during America's colonial period. In a passage from his book *The Adventures of Daniel Boone*, he describes his feelings about the settlement of the area that would become the state of Kentucky:

> *Here, where the hand of violence shed the blood of the innocent; where the horrid yells of savages, and the groans of the distressed, sounded in our ears, we now hear the praises and adorations of our Creator; where wretched wigwams stood, the miserable abode of savages, we behold the foundations of cities laid, that, in all probability, will equal the glory of the greatest upon earth.*

Source: Daniel Boone. "The Adventures of Daniel Boone: Chapter One." Archiving Early America. *Archiving Early America, 2013.* Web. Accessed March 21, 2013.

Changing Minds

In this excerpt, Boone states his opinion that Kentucky has been improved by white settlers. This was a common belief at the time. But many people feel that it was wrong for white settlers to move into Native American lands. Take a stand on this issue. Imagine that a friend holds the opposite opinion. Use two or three pieces of evidence to explain your position to your friend.

CHAPTER TWO

A DIVERSE LAND

From 2.5 million years ago until approximately 16,000 years ago, glaciers covered the northern part of North America. The movement and melting of these ice sheets created much of this continent's geography. North America has one of the most varied landscapes in the world.

Rocky Mountain National Park in Colorado, United States, has ecosystems that range from wooded forests to mountain tundra and is home to a variety of wildlife.

Sumidero Canyon in the Mexican state of Chiapas has walls up to 2,600 feet (792 m) high.

North American Mountains

North America's Rocky Mountains stretch from Northern Alberta and British Columbia in Canada to the state of New Mexico in the western United States. They are more than 3,000 miles (4,800 km) long. In some places this mountain range is more than 300 miles (483 km) wide. The Rockies' highest point is Mount Elbert in the state of Colorado, at 14,433 feet (4,389 m).

The Appalachian Mountains are located in eastern Canada and the United States. They are almost 2,000 miles (3,219 km) long. Their highest point is Mount Mitchell in the state of North Carolina, at 6,684 feet (2,037 m).

Mexico is home to three major mountain ranges. They are the Sierra Madre Occidental in the west, the Sierra Madre Oriental in the east, and the Sierra Madre del Sur in the south. The highest point in Mexico is Pico de Orizaba. This dormant volcano rises 18,406 feet (5,636 m).

The city of Quebec, Canada, overlooks the icy water of the Saint Lawrence River.

Bodies of Water

North America has many freshwater lakes and long rivers. Glaciers carved the Great Lakes. They are located in Canada and the United States. Lakes Superior, Michigan, Huron, Erie, and Ontario make up the Great Lakes. Combined, they have the largest freshwater surface area anywhere in the world.

The Mississippi River is the largest river in North America. It starts in Lake Itasca in the state of Minnesota and flows south all the way to the Gulf of Mexico. It is 2,350 miles (3,782 km) long.

A Varied Climate

There are many different climates in North America. Much of North America is part of a temperate zone. This means that the weather is usually not very hot or very cold. These areas have four distinct seasons. Southern Canada and much of the United States are part of this temperate climate. This means they have hot and humid summers and cold winters.

The Great Salt Lake

The Great Salt Lake in the US state of Utah is the largest salt-water lake in the Western Hemisphere. This lake's size tends to change a great deal every year. But in an average year, it covers 950 to 1,500 square miles (2,460 to 3,885 sq km). The Great Salt Lake is actually far saltier than seawater. It is almost impossible for anything to live in such salty water. But the area surrounding the lake is home to a variety of birds, including bald eagles.

Greenland and the Canadian Shield experience cool to very cold temperatures. The Canadian Shield includes eastern, central, and northwestern Canada, as well as parts of the northern United States. Some of the land in this area is permanently frozen or under snow and ice for most of the year.

A massive ice sheet covers much of Greenland. Two-thirds of this island nation is actually above the Arctic Circle. There is not much rainfall there. Greenland is very dry.

Much of Mexico and the southern and mid-Pacific coast of the United States are part of a dry climate. These areas see very little rainfall.

The Mississippi River

The Mississippi River is an important waterway. It is the fourth-largest river in the world. It flows slowly through the United States for 2,350 miles (3,782 km). It borders on or flows through ten American states. People have used the river to travel and move goods for hundreds of years. The Mississippi River has played an important role in American history, art, and music.

The Mississippi River

The Mississippi River is a water source as well as a source of employment and industry for the cities along its path. How do you think the major cities located on the Mississippi have been affected by their location on the river? Why do you think the river has been so important to the economy and history of the United States?

Central America is very different from the rest of North America. Most of Central America has a humid, tropical climate. Temperatures stay above 64 degrees Fahrenheit (18°C) all year. Central America receives a lot of rain.

CHAPTER THREE

FROM FOREST LIFE TO DESERT HABITATS

With so many habitats and climates, it is no wonder that many plants and animals call North America home.

Boreal Forests

Boreal forests are home to spruce and balsam fir trees. These forests are found in North America from the Aleutian Islands to Alaska and northern Canada.

Squirrel monkeys live in the tropical rainforests of Costa Rica and Panama in Central America.

A male caribou stands among fall-colored tundra plants in Denali National Park, Alaska, United States.

Caribou are a species of reindeer that live in the boreal forests of North America. They live and travel in huge herds. Caribou can survive the cold climate of the Arctic Circle. They have thick fur that keeps them warm. Timber wolves are the main predators in boreal forests. They often hunt caribou. Timber wolves travel in packs. These packs are led by a mated male and female pair.

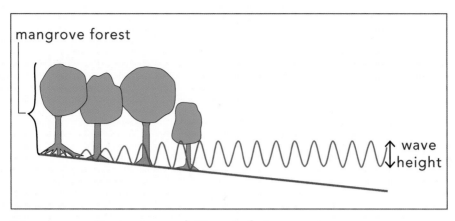

Mangrove Forests and Coastal Areas

People who live near coasts are at risk from extreme weather events such as hurricanes. Many scientists believe that global climate change will cause more frequent and stronger storms. Mangrove forests can help protect people from these events by reducing the height of waves as they come ashore. Scientists have found that traveling through at least 328 feet (100 m) of mangrove trees can reduce wave height by up to 66 percent. But mangrove forests are in danger due to pollution. How might the loss of mangrove forests harm people in coastal areas?

Mangrove Forests

Mangrove forests are home to oak, palm, and mangrove trees. These swampy areas are located in the lowlands of Mexico and southern Florida. Alligators and many species of poisonous snakes call these swamps home. Mangroves grow best in areas with a lot of water. They are often found where rainforests and oceans meet. These trees have roots that grow above the ground. They look as if they are on stilts.

Tropical Rainforests

Tropical rainforests cover much of southern Mexico and Central America. These forests are home to tall trees that form a canopy. Under the canopy is another level of plant life. This includes plants such as tree ferns, gum trees, and mangrove trees. There are many different kinds of tropical birds in the rainforest. Monkeys are also common in Central America.

Deserts and Grasslands

The United States and Mexico are home to deserts and grasslands. In

Prairie Dogs

Prairie dogs live in North American grasslands. They are rodents with short legs and strong claws. Prairie dogs create burrow systems below the ground. These burrows have many entrances and tunnels. Prairie dogs live in colonies. The largest recorded prairie dog colony was found in Texas. Approximately 400 million prairie dogs lived there.

Prairie dogs are native to North America's grasslands, ranging from Canada to Mexico. This mother and her two young are peering out of their underground burrow.

the western United States and northern Mexico, there are many kinds of cacti. Animals that live in these desert areas are often nocturnal. Tall grasses cover the prairies, or grasslands, of the Great Plains. This area lies west of the Mississippi River and east of the Rocky Mountains in the United States and Canada.

Threatened Species

Habitat destruction and pollution have driven many North American plants and animals to the edge of extinction. Canada's burrowing owl is one such

Sequoia Trees

Giant sequoia trees grow only on the western slopes of the Sierra Nevada Mountains in the US state of California. They grow to an average height of 160 to 279 feet (50 to 85 m). The oldest known giant sequoia was 3,500 years old. The coastal redwood grows along the northern California coast. At up to 367 feet (112 m) tall, they are the tallest trees in the world. These trees have been highly prized for their wood. Without efforts by preservation groups, people would long ago have harvested every last old coastal redwood.

animal. Burrowing owls live in prairie grasslands. They travel each year from Canada to their winter habitats in the southeast United States and Mexico. Conservation groups are working to save the burrowing owl.

The Great Plains were once home to the American bison. Today the bison and antelope that used to live in these areas are almost extinct due to mass hunting.

The giant sequoias of Sequoia National Park dwarf the many people who come to visit this area.

FURTHER EVIDENCE

Chapter Three covers some of the threatened species of North America. What was one of the main points of this information? What is the main point the chapter is making about the causes of extinction among plants and animals in North America? Check out the Web site at the link below. Choose a quote from the Web site that relates to this chapter. Does this quote support the author's main point? Does it make a new point?

Endangered Species of North America

www.mycorelibrary.com/north-america

THE MANY PEOPLES OF NORTH AMERICA

North America is home to many different peoples and cultures. Many Europeans came here in search of a better life. Many native people were here long before Columbus.

Before Colonization

Inuits are native people of Greenland, Canada, and Alaska. They ate animals such as seals and whales.

This young woman from Canada's Squamish Nation is wearing ceremonial clothing as part of the nation's annual Powwow.

The Maya people who once lived in modern-day Belize in Central America left behind stunning ruins, including this site, known as Tikal.

Some Inuits still practice their traditional culture and hunting. But many now live in modern cities.

The Maya were one of the native peoples of Mexico and Guatemala. More than 5 million people spoke a Mayan language before Spanish explorers came to North America. The Maya built great cities and temples. They also had systems of mathematics and timekeeping. Maya still live in North America today.

The land that is now Canada and the United States was home to many different native societies before the arrival of Europeans. Some of these people hunted and gathered their food. Others farmed and raised livestock. Some were nomadic, meaning they moved from place to place. Others lived in permanent villages.

After the arrival of settlers, European illnesses killed many native people. Because they had never been exposed to these diseases, they did not have immunity. Immunity is the ability to resist a disease or illness. Settlers eager to create farmland also drove many native people out of their homelands. The American and Canadian governments often helped to force native people from their land.

Today many native cultures throughout North America have begun to celebrate their history and traditions once again.

Carnival and Mardi Gras

Carnival is a festive holiday that falls immediately before the Christian season of Lent, which leads up to the Easter holiday. In Central America and the Caribbean Islands, Carnival is often celebrated with parades, costumes, and music and dancing. In the United States and other parts of the world, people call this holiday Mardi Gras.

Life in Canada

Most of Canada's provinces were once a part of French and English colonies. Many French and English traditions are still common in Canada.

Canada is known for its health care system. When Canadians see a doctor or go to the hospital, they do not have to pay. Everyone pays

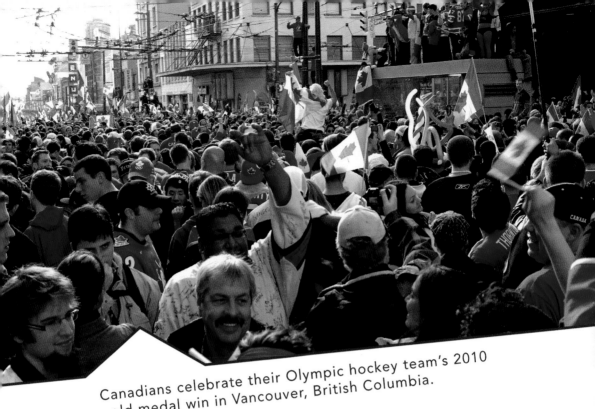

Canadians celebrate their Olympic hockey team's 2010 gold medal win in Vancouver, British Columbia.

a certain amount of money for health care through taxes.

Ice hockey is one of the most popular sports in Canada. Canadian hockey teams play in the United States' National Hockey League (NHL). Other winter sports are also popular.

The American Melting Pot

The United States has a unique culture due to its history of immigration. Many people have come to

Día de los Muertos

Día de los Muertos, or Day of the Dead, is a Mexican holiday on which people remember friends and family members who have died. Mexicans celebrate this national holiday on November 1 and 2. Families often spend this day caring for graves. They also prepare special altars to honor the dead. They offer candy skulls, marigold flowers, and favorite foods and drinks as gifts to the dead. Many Mexican Americans also celebrate Día de los Muertos.

America from all over the world in search of a better life. Other Americans are descendants of people who were brought there by force as slaves from Africa.

One of the most popular holidays in the United States is Independence Day. Most Americans call this holiday the Fourth of July. Independence Day honors the signing of the Declaration of Independence. This document declared the United States to be independent from Great Britain. On Independence Day, Americans enjoy fireworks, parades, and barbecues.

EXPLORE ONLINE

Chapter Four talks about the early history of North America. The Web site below also focuses on this topic. As you know, every source is different. How is the information on the Web site different from the information in this chapter? What information is the same? How do the two sources present information differently? What can you learn from this Web site?

America after Columbus

www.mycorelibrary.com/north-america

Viva la Mexico!

Mexico is home to many native people as well as people of Spanish descent. Mexico was once a Spanish colony. Each year in September, Mexicans celebrate the *Fiesta Patrias,* or Festival of Independence. This holiday lasts for several days. It features huge parades and fireworks. Religion is also an important part of Mexico's culture. Many Mexicans are Catholic.

CHAPTER FIVE

NORTH AMERICA TODAY

Today democratically elected officials govern most North American countries. The United States is a federal republic governed by a constitution. The government is made up of a president, a congress, and a Supreme Court. Mexico is also a federal republic. Canada is a part of the British Commonwealth of Nations. But British power in

Parliament Hill in the city of Ottawa in the province of Ontario is home to Canada's parliament, the nation's lawmaking body.

Many Central American children, such as these schoolgirls in Panama, live in poverty.

Canada is limited by a constitution. An elected prime minister leads Canada's government.

Speaking Many Languages

With so many immigrants from all over the world, North America is home to people who speak many different languages. The United States has no official language. But most Americans speak English. However, today more than 10 percent of people in the United States speak Spanish. Canada is a bilingual country. This means it has two official languages,

French and English.
Spanish is the official
language of Mexico.

Climate Change

Many countries around
the world are beginning
to experience the effects
of global climate change.
Greenland is one of the
fastest-warming places on
the planet. Greenland's
ice is now melting more
quickly than ever before.

Poverty in North America

Many parts of North America are very wealthy compared to the rest of the world. But many of the people of Mexico, Central America, and the Caribbean live in poverty. For example, 39 percent of households in Latin America and the Caribbean live in poverty. Many people from these countries immigrate to the United States in search of a better life for their families.

Most experts agree the United States is one
of the world's biggest producers of pollutants. To
decrease the pollution it produces, the United States
is working on new ways to create power and to
use power more efficiently. More and more North
Americans are trying to reduce the amount of energy
and natural resources they use.

Many North Americans are trying to find ways to use less energy and create less pollution. Technology such as these solar panels in the US Mojave Desert helps this effort.

Facing the Future

North America has problems to solve in the coming years. These include pollution and improving the lives of its less-fortunate people. But from the frozen lands of the north to the tropical rainforests of Central America, the many peoples of North America are proud to call this continent home.

The Statue of Liberty in New York Harbor is a symbol of hope for many immigrants to the United States. The poem "The New Colossus" by Emma Lazarus, from which this excerpt is taken, is carved at the base of the statue:

> *"Keep ancient lands, your storied pomp!" cries she*
> *With silent lips. "Give me your tired, your poor,*
> *Your huddled masses yearning to breathe free,*
> *The wretched refuse of your teeming shore.*
>
> *Send these, the homeless, tempest-tost to me,*
> *I lift my lamp beside the golden door!"*

Source: Emma Lazarus. "The New Colossus." POETS.org. The Academy of American Poets, 2013. Web. Accessed April 12, 2013.

Nice View

What do you think Lazurus's famous poem meant to Americans when she wrote it in 1883? How do you think Americans feel about immigration today? Imagine that you and a friend are discussing immigration. One of you agrees with the ideas of this poem, while the other does not. Write a brief essay explaining your and your friend's opinions. Be sure to state both of your positions and include evidence to support both of your views.

Toronto's skyline at night

Toronto

Toronto is on the shore of Lake Ontario. It is the most populated city in Canada. There are more than 100 languages spoken in Toronto.

Lake Atitlan

Lake Atitlan is a volcanic lake in Guatemala. Surrounded by three volcanoes, it is the deepest lake in Central America.

Lake Atitlan and one of its three volcanoes

New York City

New York City, New York, is the biggest city in the United States. It is home to many famous landmarks and immigrants from around the world.

New York City's Times Square

Mexico City's Fine Arts Museum

A green sea turtle in the ocean near Nassau, Bahamas

One view of the enormous Grand Canyon

Mexico City

Mexico City is the capital of Mexico and the largest city in North America. It is also one of the oldest cities in the Western Hemisphere.

Nassau

Nassau is the capital of the tropical nation the Bahamas, one of the world's most popular vacation destinations.

The Grand Canyon

The Grand Canyon, in the state of Arizona in the United States, is known for its awe-inspiring size and beauty. Visitors flock to the Grand Canyon from around the world to experience this natural wonder.

Why Do I Care?

Chapter Three discusses some of the many plants and animals found in North America. It also talks about how pollution and habitat destruction have harmed some animal communities. Does damage to the environment have an effect on your life as well? How do you think global climate change could change your day-to-day activities?

Take a Stand

This book talks about the growing importance of the Spanish language in the United States. Some people believe that the government should print important documents in Spanish as well as English. Others think only English should be used in official government business. Do you think the United States' government should make its documents bilingual? Why or why not? Write a few sentences explaining your opinion.

You Are There

Imagine that you are a European explorer reaching North America for the first time. What natural features or plants and animals might you find most surprising? How might any indigenous people you encounter react to your presence? Write 300 words describing your experiences.

Say What?

Studying North America can mean learning a lot of new vocabulary. Find five words in this book you've never seen or heard before. Use a dictionary to find out what they mean. Then write the meanings in your own words, and use each word in a new sentence.

GLOSSARY

bilingual
able to speak two languages

colonial
relating to the period of time during which much of North America was controlled and colonized by European countries and settlers, and more specifically to the 13 British colonies that eventually became the United States of America

conservation
preservation, protection, or restoration of the natural environment, natural ecosystems, vegetation, and wildlife

culture
the beliefs, behaviors, and other characteristics of a particular group of people

economy
all the products and trade of a country

extinct
no longer existing

immigrant
a person who has left one country to live in another

indigenous
originating or occurring naturally in a particular place; native

industry
the making of materials into goods that can be sold

nocturnal
sleeping during the day and awake at night

LEARN MORE

Books

Aloian, Molly. *Explore North America.* New York: Crabtree, 2007.

Dennis, Yvonne Wakim. *Children of Native America Today.* Watertown, MA: Charlesbridge, 2003.

Jackson, Tom. *Animals, Birds, & Fish of North America.* Leicester, UK: Anness, 2012.

Web Links

To learn more about North America, visit ABDO Publishing Company online at **www.abdopublishing.com**. Web sites about North America are featured on our Book Links page. These links are routinely monitored and updated to provide the most current information available.

Visit **www.mycorelibrary.com** for free additional tools for teachers and students.

INDEX

ABOUT THE AUTHOR

Emily C. Koenig grew up in rural Minnesota. She graduated from the University of St. Thomas in Saint Paul, Minnesota. Today she is a writer, blogger, editor, and avid traveler. Her travels hold some of her favorite memories.